GUIDEL

Lay Leader/ Lay Member

Connecting Your
Congregation and
Your Annual Conference

Sandy Jackson
General Board of Discipleship

LAY LEADER/LAY MEMBER

Copyright © 2012 by Cokesbury

Some paragraph numbers for and language in the Book of Discipline *may have changed in the 2012 revision, which was published after these Guidelines were printed. We regret any inconvenience.*

Contents

Called to a Ministry of Faithfulness and Vitality

You are so important to the life of the Christian church! You have consented to join with other people of faith who, through the millennia, have sustained the church by extending God's love to others. You have been called and have committed your unique passions, gifts, and abilities to a position of leadership. This Guideline will help you understand the basic elements of that ministry within your own church and within The United Methodist Church.

Leadership in Vital Ministry

Each person is called to ministry by virtue of his or her baptism, and that ministry takes place in all aspects of daily life, both in and outside of the church. Your leadership role requires that you will be a faithful participant in the **mission of the church,** which is to partner with God to **make disciples of Jesus Christ for the transformation of the world.** You will not only engage in your area of ministry, but will also work to empower others to be in ministry as well. The vitality of your church, and the Church as a whole, depends upon the faith, abilities, and actions of all who work together for the glory of God.

Clearly then, as a pastoral leader or leader among the laity, your ministry is not just a "job," but a spiritual endeavor. You are a spiritual leader now, and others will look to you for spiritual leadership. What does this mean?

All persons who follow Jesus are called to grow spiritually through the practice of various Christian habits (or "means of grace") such as prayer, Bible study, private and corporate worship, acts of service, Christian conferencing, and so on. Jesus taught his disciples practices of spiritual growth and leadership that you will model as you guide others. As members of the congregation grow through the means of grace, they will assume their own role in ministry and help others in the same way. This is the cycle of disciple making.

The Church's Vision

While there is one mission—to make disciples of Jesus Christ—the portrait of a successful mission will differ from one congregation to the next. One of your roles is to listen deeply for the guidance and call of God in your own context. In your church, neighborhood, or greater community, what are the greatest needs? How is God calling your congregation to be in a ministry of service and witness where they are? What does vital ministry look like in the life of your congregation and its neighbors? What are the characteristics, traits, and actions that identify a person as a faithful disciple in your context? This portrait, or vision, is formed when you and the other leaders discern together how your gifts from God come together to fulfill the will of God.

Assessing Your Efforts

We are generally good at deciding what to do, but we sometimes skip the more important first question of what we want to accomplish. Knowing your task (the mission of disciple making) and knowing what results you want (the vision of your church) are the first two steps in a vital ministry. The third step is in knowing how you will assess or measure the results of what you do and who you are (and become) because of what you do. Those measures relate directly to mission and vision, and they are more than just numbers.

One of your leadership tasks will be to take a hard look, with your team, at all the things your ministry area does or plans to do. No doubt they are good and worthy activities; the question is, *"Do these activities and experiences lead people into a mature relationship with God and a life of deeper discipleship?"* That is the business of the church, and the church needs to do what only the church can do. You may need to eliminate or alter some of what you do if it does not measure up to the standard of faithful disciple making. It will be up to your ministry team to establish the specific standards against which you compare all that you do and hope to do. (This Guideline includes further help in establishing goals, strategies, and measures for this area of ministry.)

The Mission of The United Methodist Church

Each local church is unique, yet it is a part of a *connection,* a living organism of the body of Christ. Being a connectional Church means in part that all United Methodist churches are interrelated through the structure and organization of districts, conferences, and jurisdictions in the larger "family" of the denomination. *The Book of Discipline of The United Methodist Church* describes, among other things, the ministry of all United Methodist Christians, the essence of servant ministry and leadership, how to organize and accomplish that ministry, and how our connectional structure works (see especially ¶¶126–138).

Our Church extends way beyond your doorstep; it is a global Church with both local and international presence. You are not alone. The resources of the entire denomination are intended to assist you in ministry. With this help and the partnership of God and one another, the mission continues. You are an integral part of God's church and God's plan!

(For help in addition to this Guideline and the *Book of Discipline*, see "Resources" at the end of your Guideline, www.umc.org, and the other websites listed on the inside back cover.)

Called to Love and Serve

"... all Christians are called to minister wherever Christ would have them serve and witness in deeds and words that heal and free" (The Book of Discipline of The United Methodist Church, ¶128).

thank you for accepting the call to be the lay leader of your congregation or lay member of annual conference! God has called you, through your church's charge conference, to serve the church in an important way. The roles of lay leader and lay member of annual conference are separate but should be complementary.

The Responsibilities of Lay Leader/ Lay Member

Responsibilities of both the lay leader and the lay member to annual conference are
- interpreting the actions and programs of the annual conference and the general church
- communicating the vision and needs of the local church to the annual conference and general church

These two roles are complementary, yet there are responsibilities unique to each role. The greatest distinction is the connections they forge with and on behalf of the congregation. The **lay leader** has a primary focus in linking the local church and community. The **lay member of annual conference** has a primary focus in linking the local church to the connectional United Methodist Church and God's worldwide church.

The *Book of Discipline* defines your role as lay leader and/or lay member and defines in broad terms the work of your congregation, the annual conference, and The United Methodist Church. Two sections will be particularly helpful for your leadership. The paragraphs in the 200s relate to the local church; ¶251.1 refers to the lay leader and ¶251.2 refers to the lay member to annual conference. Paragraph 602.4 also contains references to the lay member of annual conference. The *Discipline* states that both the lay leader and lay member must be professing members of the local church. The lay members to annual conference must be professing members for the two years preceding their election and active participants in The United Methodist Church for at least four years before their election (¶ 602.4), though that requirement may be waived for persons under 30. Both are elected by the charge conference, however the lay member(s) to annual conference may be elected annually or each quadrennium (depending on the charge conference rules).

The *Discipline* recommends that the lay leader be **one** of the lay members of annual conference. This is because the lay leader is to serve as interpreter to the congregation the actions of the annual conference and the general Church (¶ 251.1 c). To be equipped for this responsibility it will be helpful for the lay leader to be a lay member to annual conference. If the lay leader is not a lay member to annual conference the two people should confer and work together as they serve. A large membership church may have several people sharing these responsibilities, but it may be difficult for the lay leader to be the sole lay member from a congregation due to the increased responsibilities of serving in both roles.

The *Discipline* has a table of contents and a topical index to help you find other items related to your role. Ask your pastor for a current copy or purchase a copy through Cokesbury (see Resources at the back of this Guideline).

The Book of Discipline of The United Methodist Church sets forth the constitution, theology, history, Wesleyan heritage, polity, plans, process, and laws by which United Methodists govern themselves. In addition to the legislation that governs our life together, it has important information regarding the mission and ministry of the church, including the General Rules of the Wesleyan societies.

Most of the book is organized by paragraph rather than page, chapter, or section. The paragraphs are numbered consecutively within each chapter or section, but numbers may be skipped between sections to allow for future additions. The *Discipline* can be modified only by a General Conference, comprised of delegates elected from each annual conference, held every four years. The General Conference "amends, perfects, clarifies, and adds its own contribution to the *Discipline*" (page v).

The Role of the Lay Leader

the responsibilities that are listed in the *Discipline* for lay leaders apply to congregations of every size and multiple point charges. However, these responsibilities are lived out with a great deal of variation among local churches. In larger congregations associate lay leaders may be elected to assist the lay leader. For example, an associate lay leader may attend specific committee meetings in place of the lay leader, be responsible for advising the congregation of continuing education opportunities, or other functions as decided.

Responsibilities of the Lay Leader

The lay leader has a role and responsibility that touches the entire breadth of the congregation's life. The lay leader

- functions as the primary lay representative of the laity in a local church
- fosters the role of the laity in mission and ministry
- meets regularly with the pastor
- is a member of the charge conference, church council, and other committees
- continues to be involved in study and training opportunities
- assists in advising the church council
- informs the laity of training opportunities

REPRESENTING THE LAITY

The lay leader serves as primary advocate for and representative of the laity in the congregation. A part of this advocacy work includes the recognition that the lay leader should be a person of faith and integrity. As an "extension" of the congregation in the community, the lay leader also will need to be aware of the reputation the church has in the community and work either to enhance it or improve it. The lay leader is also an advocate for the needs of the community; to inspire the congregation to care for those beyond the walls and windows of the church.

MODELING DISCIPLESHIP

Although this is not specifically required by the *Discipline,* one current emphasis is on the vital personal faith of leaders within the church. Your visibility as the lay leader in the congregation places you in a position to model good habits of personal devotion and discipleship. As you engage in spiritual practices and serve in outreach and mission, you serve as an example and mentor to others. As a disciple and leader, you should participate in a disciplined group such as a Covenant Discipleship group or class meeting.

Wesleyan Class Meetings
The Wesleyan Class Meetings were more than the small groups who gather today for self-help, book reading, or Bible study. The class meetings of early Methodism focused on developing "holiness of heart and life" and "watching over one another with love" or holding each other accountable for their discipleship. These groups found their life by living the disciplines (means of grace) rather than living by legislation, which so often governs our current life together in the *Book of Discipline*.

FOSTERING THE ROLE OF THE LAITY
The role of laity must be renewed and expanded if your congregation is to be a vital organism. Our Methodist heritage includes active lay leadership and involvement in spreading scriptural and social holiness throughout the land. It is your responsibility to encourage other laity to use their spiritual gifts to love and serve God and neighbor.

In addition, you can help to foster awareness of the ministry of the laity through their ministry in the home, workplace, community, and the world. In part of the section on "The Meaning of Membership" in the *Discipline*, ¶220 describes *The Call to Ministry of All the Baptized*. This paragraph explains that each member is a servant of Christ in mission in the local and worldwide community. You can foster the awareness of the laity in their responsibilities as members by calling their attention to this important paragraph. Assist church members to discover and use their spiritual gifts to strengthen the church and to witness to persons in all areas of their lives. Encourage church members to use their skills—such as carpentry, plumbing, teaching, tax preparation, nursing, business, and so on—to help each other or persons in the community and throughout the world.

RECOGNIZE AND CELEBRATE THE MINISTRY OF THE LAITY
Bringing awareness of the role of the laity to the congregation and community can be accomplished by finding ways within the community of faith to recognize and celebrate all the ministries of the laity. Here are some suggestions.
- Observe Laity Sunday, annually; usually the third Sunday of October.
- Invite community groups such as fire fighters, teachers, or city workers to worship and recognize their work as ministry.
- Recognize laity who have become lay servants (formerly lay speakers) and announce training events for all laity.
- Prepare visual displays that celebrate the ministries of the laity within the walls of the church and in the world outside the building.

- Regularly promote special opportunities for service and mission projects.
- Recognize the steady ministry of groups and individuals who live out their faith in service by regularly volunteering in schools and the community.

You can provide opportunities for people of all ages to respond to how they have lived as faithful Christians during the past week, including in the workplace. They might share those experiences in worship, small groups, newsletters, or bulletins.

MEETING WITH THE PASTOR

The *Book of Discipline* states that the mission of the Church is to make disciples of Jesus Christ for the transformation of the world. Each congregation must discern the way to accomplish that mission in its unique setting. And each pastor and lay leader must decide how they will share the work as *together* they guide the congregation in accomplishing its mission.

You will want to meet regularly with the pastor to discuss the state of the congregation and the needs for ministry both within and beyond the congregation. Cultivating a healthy relationship with the pastor is a vital part of your ministry, and being the healthy bridge between the pastor(s) and congregation is essential.

Paragraph 131 of the *Book of Discipline* talks about The Unity of Ministry: "There is but one ministry in Christ, but there are diverse gifts and evidences of God's grace in the body of Christ (Ephesians 4:4-16). The ministry of all Christians is complementary. *No ministry is subservient to another.* All United Methodists are summoned and sent by Christ to live and work together in *mutual interdependence* and to be guided by the Spirit into the truth that frees and the love that reconciles" (emphasis added).

This way of being in ministry together is not new. It was practiced by the first-century church with overwhelming success in making disciples for Jesus Christ! It is a clarion call for clergy and laity to work together in ways that have been forgotten or disregarded in the past few centuries. One way to demonstrate this working relationship is that the lay leader can be physically present as co-leader with the appointed leader in meetings, worship, and the community.

LEADERSHIP COVENANT

A good way to work together is to establish a covenant between you (pastor and lay leader) regarding how you will work together to carry out your tasks and responsibilities.

Leadership Covenant Sample

Between _____(pastor)

and

_____(lay leader)

- Description of Local Mission and Ministry Area (Local Church, District, Annual Conference). Remind one another of the history of the area; when and how established, distinctions, purpose. Write a 2-3 sentence synopsis of your discussion.
- Roles (who does what).
- Expectations (Learning actions, time lines, shared vision, goals).
- Accountability (Participation in covenant group; spiritual self care, such as days apart).
- Evaluation (Outcomes based on goals).
- Covenant Review Plan, including the date for review, how it will be done, and what will be assessed.
- Plan for improvement.
- Celebration of accomplishments.
- (See a sample covenant on the CD included in Guidelines set.)

SERVING ON VARIOUS COMMITTEES

You will be busy! The lay leader is automatically a member of charge conference, church council, finance committee, nominations and leadership development committee, and staff/pastor-parish relations committee. The lay leader represents and advocates for the laity in specific ways in each of these places. You can find out more about them by reading the Guidelines for each of these committees and their responsibilities, but here are some brief descriptions.

The **charge conference** is the connecting link between the local church and the general Church and has general oversight of the church council. The charge conference is held annually at a time set by the district superintendent. The lay leader represents the laity by
- attending the charge conference
- submitting a report on the state of lay ministry in the congregation

The **church council** is the group responsible for planning and coordinating the administrative and programmatic life of the congregation. The church council includes pastor(s) and laity who chair committees and task forces. Your role as lay leader at the church council is to
- bring a broad perspective of laity of all ages as you listen to the plans for implementing the mission and vision of the congregation

- apprise the council of needs within the neighborhood
- be prepared to interpret the plans and decisions of the church council to the laity of the congregation

The **finance committee** prepares an annual budget for the congregation to submit to the church council for review and adoption. The committee is responsible together with the stewardship committee (if you have one) for developing and implementing a plan for raising funds for the budget adopted by the church council. The committee administers the funds according to the instructions of the church council and guides the work of the church treasurer and financial secretary. Your role in this committee is similar to your role in the church council. You are to
- represent all the laity and the community as the budget is prepared and as funds are administered
- interpret the finances of the church to the congregation

The **nominations and leadership development committee** *identifies, develops, deploys, evaluates*, and *monitors* the Christian spiritual leadership of the congregation. **This is a critically important committee in the life of the congregation.** This committee should be the hub of leadership selection and training. The responsibilities include more than finding people to fill empty slots. *Identifying* is more than finding willing people; it includes discovering the gifts needed for various ministries and who possesses those gifts. *Developing* is about equipping, providing prayer support, and mentoring those who are in leadership positions. *Deploying* refers to discerning areas of mission and ministry where the gifts of the members will be used most effectively. *Evaluating* the success of each committee and the Nominations and Leadership Development committee's efforts is essential to improving the work of the congregation. *Monitoring* is done by feeling the pulse of the congregation—what needs to be added to the leadership? What should change or be eliminated?

As a representative of the laity on this committee, your role is to
- encourage the spiritual gifts assessment of the potential leaders so that they can be placed in positions where their gifts and passion will enhance their leadership
- encourage the committee to provide leadership training, mentors, and prayer partners for the committees and chairs of committees
- assist in monitoring and evaluating congregational needs for leadership and success of each ministry or mission area

Remember that leadership development and deployment is dynamic, always changing as ministry needs change and as church members join or leave the congregation. (See the Guideline *Committee on Nominations and Leadership Development*.)

The **staff/pastor-parish relations committee** reflects on the work of the pastor(s) and staff and assists them in assessing their gifts and setting priorities as they lead and serve the church. Members of this committee **other than the lay leader and lay member to annual conference** are divided into three classes with a new class elected each year for a three-year term. This committee meets at least quarterly or more often when requested. These meetings are closed sessions and meeting discussions are to be kept confidential. See ¶258.2 in the *Book of Discipline* for more information on this committee. Your role on this committee is to
- Represent the interests of the laity. What are you hearing? What is beneficial or what are the concerns?
- Support the pastor and staff in their ministry efforts; establish prayer support teams or partners, and encourage Sabbath time.

CONTINUOUSLY INVOLVED IN STUDY
It will be important for you to continue to study and attend training to understand the church's reason for existence and the types of ministry that will fulfill the church's mission faithfully and effectively. Your attendance models the importance of continuing education for other church leaders. In addition, you have the opportunity through district and conference channels to inform the laity of educational opportunities provided by the annual conference and to participate in lay training. A lay leader is urged to become a certified lay servant in order to increase skills for leadership. (See page 21 for more information on Lay Servant Ministries)

ASSIST IN ADVISING THE CHURCH COUNCIL
Your role in helping the council with the internal workings of the church is already obvious. Your role extends beyond the immediate boundaries of the church building into the community. In so doing, you can better attend to the unique ministry and mission needs in your community. You can assist the council to
- Look for and take advantage of opportunities to interpret the mission and ministry of the congregation to the community; where can the ministries of your congregation assist the community? What do you have to offer?
- Share ways in which the congregation could provide mission and ministry opportunities to meet the needs of persons in the community. Could you partner with a local elementary school, homeless shelter, sports organization? In what ways could you participate in disaster relief or neighborhood watch?

District and Conference Lay Leaders

The lay leader of a local church has counterparts in the district and annual conference who can help with the job. The district lay leader works in partnership with the district superintendent and is charged with training local church lay leaders; fostering awareness of the role of laity in congregations, workplaces, homes, and communities; and supporting and enabling lay participation in the planning and decision making of the district. The district lay leader relates to other organized groups of laity within the district, such as lay servant ministries, United Methodist Women, United Methodist Men, and United Methodist Youth.

The annual conference lay leader works in partnership with the bishop and represents the interests of laity. The conference lay leader relates to organized groups of laity to assist with planning, implementation, and evaluation of ministries of the laity. The conference lay leader is an advocate for lay ministries and also promotes the role of laity in the annual conference session.

FOR REFLECTION

For I was hungry and you gave me food, I was thirsty and you gave me something to drink, I was a stranger and you welcomed me, I was naked and you gave me clothing, I was sick and you took care of me, I was in prison and you visited me (Matthew 25:35-36).

New Hope United Methodist Church had a plan to cultivate laypersons to assist the pastor with hospital visits. A group of interested laity received training in hospital visitation, but the program never got off the ground. Why? Some members of the congregation reportedly wanted to be visited only by the pastor, not by a layperson.

- How could a lay leader have been an advocate in the congregation for the group of trained and available lay visitors?
- How could the lay leader have been an advocate in the congregation for the pastor?
- How might this Scripture passage help the lay leader interpret ministry opportunities to the congregation? What other passages could be helpful?
- What methods could the pastor and lay leader employ to bring Scripture and the church's mission to the forefront regarding shared clergy/laity ministry?

The Role of the Lay Member of Annual Conference

t he lay member of annual conference, along with the pastor, interprets the work done by the annual conference session to the congregation. They are the liaison between the congregation and the general church and represent the congregation in the actions taken at the annual conference sessions. The lay member

- Participates in the annual conference sessions and votes on all matters except those pertaining to ministerial relations.
- Reports to the congregation *in the week following the annual conference session* and *to the church council at its next meeting after the close of the conference session.* The *Discipline* states that the report to the church council must be within three months of the close of the session. (Go to "Communication Tools for Lay Members to Annual Conference" and also "The Things I Learned at Annual Conference" at http://www.gbod.org/laity.)
- Serves as a member of the staff/pastor-parish relations committee, church council, and finance committee. (See pages 11-13.)

You and the other lay members to annual conference will be serving with an equal number of clergy members. This is an opportunity to listen and learn from each other and to experience a greater variety of God's human creation than you may experience in your local congregation. You will meet and work with people from different size churches; various cultures; urban, rural, and suburban congregations; and a wide variety of professions, life experience, and economic levels. Take advantage of this opportunity by getting acquainted with people sitting near you. Celebrate the diversity of The United Methodist Church!

Annual conference covers a time span of three to five days, and most annual conferences in the United States meet in May or June. The bishop may occasionally call extra sessions if there is emergent business. Your pastor or district superintendent can inform you about meeting dates, or you can check the annual conference website.

ANNUAL CONFERENCE: TWO MEANINGS!

An *annual conference* is a unique geographic area of The United Methodist Church. Each annual conference is assigned a bishop (sometimes called the episcopal leader) and elects a conference lay leader. Shared resources (including itinerant clergy) and policies connect all local churches within the annual conference.

The *annual conference session* is the annual meeting of the lay and clergy members of the geographical area. This meeting sets directions and budget for the area, and the bishop appoints clergy members to their place of service for the next year.

Responsibilities of the Lay Member

The lay member to annual conference has many responsibilities, some before the annual conference session, others during, and still more following the session. If you are employed, you will have to take time from work to attend these gatherings. When the dates are announced, take care to plan with your employer for the necessary days of vacation. It is important that you attend the entire annual conference session.

PREPARE FOR THE ANNUAL CONFERENCE

Study the pre-conference journal and materials that are submitted for action by the annual conference. These materials may be mailed to you several weeks before annual conference or may be available on the annual conference website. To prepare, you should

- Attend any pre-conference district meetings and training sessions.
- Discover your annual conference process for conducting business. For example, some conferences operate with Robert's Rules of Order (parliamentary procedure); other conferences operate with discernment processes and consensus. Your pastor or annual conference office can help you prepare before your first session.
- Develop a general knowledge of the *Book of Discipline* (see information at the beginning of this Guideline).
- Meet with the pastor, lay leader, and congregation members to discuss issues that will be a part of the annual conference business.
- Note issues and concerns that need to be taken to the annual conference session.

PARTICIPATE DURING ANNUAL CONFERENCE

- Attend the annual conference laity session. This may be a training event, a form of information sharing, or a time to celebrate the ministry of the laity in your annual conference.
- Participate in all sessions dealing with annual conference business. During business sessions, you will be asked to vote on legislation, resolutions, reports, and budget.
- Listen to proceedings in order to make informed decisions when voting. You do not have to vote the same as other members from your congregation, and you may abstain if you do not feel qualified to vote on a particu-

lar issue. You must hold in mind the tension between the ministry of the Church in the world and the interests of your own congregation. Sometimes you might choose to vote for the "greater good" on issues that may (or may not) have a direct impact on your congregation and issues that may even increase your local church budget. Examples might be an increase in budget for mission work, work to curb violence that is not part of your local community, a position on a social issue on which all members of your congregation do not agree. In these instances, you have the role of explaining and educating your congregation about the issues.

- Participate in all worship experiences (opening worship, early morning or evening chapel, ordination, memorial service, and others). You will have opportunities to experience several worship styles, hear a variety of music groups and preachers, and join in new ways to worship God.
- Attend plenary and Bible study sessions. Annual conference sessions can be an excellent way to grow spiritually.
- Explore the resource display to gather information and ideas for ministry in your congregation. During fellowship events, at display tables, and in casual conversation you will learn about The United Methodist Church in new ways. Participate fully with anticipation of new ways God might come to you.

> **A spiritual discipline for conference is journaling!** Write your reflections about proceedings, discussions, worship experiences, special ceremonies, music, and so on as preparation for later sharing with your congregation. Keep an accurate record of the votes taken that will have impact on the congregation's finances, operations, and ministry.

SERVE AFTER ANNUAL CONFERENCE
Attendance at the annual conference session is the basis for the work you will do in your congregation throughout the year.

- Share information with your congregation about your experience. Remember that the report to the congregation is to be given within the following week and the report to the church council at the next meeting or no later than three months after the annual conference session.
- Search websites and general Church news sources and your annual conference newspaper for information to share with your congregation throughout the year.
- You may also choose to participate in annual conference or district committees or work areas.

General Conference
Every four years all of the annual conferences, along with the central and missionary conferences, meet together to review and enact new legislation

or approve new initiatives of The United Methodist Church. This conference is held in the years divisible by four (2008, 2012, 2016...).The year before, each annual conference elects lay and clergy delegates to represent them at General Conference. Typically, lay members to conference indicate a willingness to be nominated for General Conference, though each annual conference has slightly different preparation and requirements of potential delegates in these elections. Check with your annual conference regarding the process to follow.

This is no easy task! It takes two weeks of your time that does not include the meetings held in your annual conference prior to General Conference. The General Conference reimburses for travel, lodging, and meals but this may not meet all of your expenses. There is a huge amount of reading required and spiritual preparation and discernment are needed in order to be prepared to serve in this role. However it is a unique experience of Christian conferencing on a grand scale.

FOR REFLECTION

Put these things into practice, devote yourself to them, so that all may see your progress (1 Timothy 4:15).

One new lay member to annual conference discovered that there was much more to conference than she had expected. The reports she had heard from other attendees gave her the impression that annual conference might be boring and more like a burden than a privilege. When she attended annual conference personally, she discovered inspiring pageantry, worship, and music. Annual conference had a spiritual aspect that had never been mentioned. Members engaged one another in Christian practices, not only in worship but also in the celebration of and decisions about their ministries.

- As you review and anticipate the different ways you will participate during annual conference, be thinking of how you can relate those different aspects of annual conference so that others can understand the whole experience.
- Think of various Christian practices (prayer, corporate worship, small group devotions, Communion, Christian conferencing, service and other acts of justice, compassion and works of mercy, and so on). How might you describe your own experiences through the lens of one or more Christian practices?

Improving Your Leadership

Preparation for leadership is not just accomplished by taking a course or reading a book. It is a lifelong process of study, prayer, and discernment. It includes developing your spiritual practices, communication skills, people skills, and administrative skills. Leadership development is a continuous improvement process!

Servant Leadership

A servant leader has certain characteristics. Jesus told the disciples, *"You know that the rulers of the Gentiles lord it over them, and their high officials exercise authority over them. Not so with you. Instead, whoever wants to become great among you must be your servant, and whoever wants to be first must be your slave—just as the Son of Man did not come to be served, but to serve, and to give his life as a ransom for many"* (Matthew 20:25-28, NIV). When you recognize the worth of others, you realize that when you perform even the most menial of tasks, you exhibit the qualities of a servant leader.

All persons who are called to Christian spiritual leadership are called to servanthood. This is the kind of leadership modeled by our leader, Jesus. When you lead by serving, you empower others in the congregation. Your leadership is lived out in a variety of ways. Sometimes you are giving directions or leading a meeting. Many times you are listening to what others say in verbal and non-verbal ways. Other times you are encouraging others to take action. Always you are ready and willing to do whatever must be done—no task is too menial for a servant leader! That doesn't mean that you have to do everything by yourself but you should be willing to do any task no matter how seemingly insignificant it may be. We may be gifted and set apart as leaders but never set above.

Spiritual Disciplines

"O begin! Fix some part of every day for private exercises... Whether you like it or no, read and pray daily. It is for your life; there is no other way: else you will be a trifler all your days." —John Wesley

John Wesley wrote these words to an itinerant preacher to encourage him in his devotional life and to stress the importance of a life focused on devotion to God. In this way, a relationship is cultivated with God. In sermons and in letters, John Wesley encouraged everyone to practice what he called the means of grace; those practices that open the way for God's grace in our lives. He believed these practices should be a part of daily life. He did not see the disciplines as Church laws but as the way of discipleship. John Wesley believed that the spiritual disciplines were more than just Bible study and prayer.

Today, Christian leaders must cultivate their relationship with God in order to lead others in spiritual growth. Spiritual leadership comes only from the overflow of our relationship with God. Without daily renewal and guidance, leaders can go astray from God's purposes and often suffer burnout. Every leader in the church should be spiritually equipped to lead.

WESLEYAN MEANS OF GRACE

Wesley talked about the practices that keep us close and in right relationship with God. He called these practices the means of grace. They are spiritual practices that keep us centered in Christ and help us to maintain "holiness of heart and life."

- **Prayer:** according to Wesley, is "the grand means of drawing near to God"
- **Bible reading:** worshipful reading is different than reading to prepare a lesson or sermon
- **Fasting or abstinence:** practicing various forms of self-denial gives priority to spiritual matters
- **Holy Communion or Eucharist:** Wesley urged Communion as often as possible
- **Christian conferencing:** remember that God is present for discernment and guidance in your conversations
- **Worship:** praise and thank God for who God is and what God has done
- **Family devotions:** attend to personal devotions outside of the public worship settings
- **Works of piety:** attend to acts of compassion and devotion
- **Works of mercy:** attend to acts of justice and service

ACCOUNTABILITY—COVENANT DISCIPLESHIP

One way to maintain this practice of spiritual disciplines or means of grace is to join or form a covenant discipleship group. Covenant discipleship is not a new concept. It began with the early Christians and was reignited with the Methodist class meeting—the small group meetings from early Methodism. John Wesley described the Methodist societies and classes in this way; "a company of men (and women) 'having the form, and seeking the power of godliness.'" In weekly meetings the members of the group help each other become more faithful in their discipleship. (See Resources for other helps for leader development, spiritual formation, and spiritual growth.)

Spiritual Gifts

God gives each believer certain abilities and gifts to prepare her or him for ministry. These gifts enable us to make unique contributions to the church, our society, and the world. In 1 Corinthians 12:4-6, Paul says, "Now there are varieties of gifts, but the same Spirit; and there are varieties of services, but the same Lord; and there are varieties of activities, but it is the same God who activates all of them in everyone." Just as we were saved by grace, so God prepares us by grace and empowers us for meaningful service.

All spiritual gifts are valuable and equally important, according to 1 Corinthians 12. Spiritual gifts are truly from God and are to be used for God's glory. Remember that natural talents are not necessarily the same as spiritual gifts, but any talents and skills can be used to glorify God. Various spiritual gifts are listed three places in the New Testament: Romans 12:6-8; 1 Corinthians 12:4-11, 27-28; and Ephesians 4:11-13.

As you begin and continue in leadership, you will want to
- use a spiritual gifts assessment tool to discover your gifts
- discover the area of ministry you are passionate about
- seek out ways to use your spiritual gifts
- thank God as you receive and/or recognize your spiritual gifts

> As you (lay leader) work with the committee on nominations and leadership development, encourage them to organize spiritual gifts workshops for the congregation in order to help members discover their gifts and passion for ministry. Resources are suggested at the end of this Guideline.

Lay Servant (Formerly "Speaking") Ministries

The *Book of Discipline* recommends that a lay leader be a certified lay speaker. The apostle Paul prepared many years for his ministry (Galatians 2:1), and we must continue to prepare for ours. In 1 Corinthians 9:25, Paul reminds us, "Everyone who competes in the games goes into strict training. They do it to get a crown that will not last; but we do it to get a crown that will last forever" (NIV). Lay servant ministry is a United Methodist system for lay leadership development. The basic and advanced courses are designed to help persons develop their skills in leadership, communication, and care-giving. Participating in this training helps you build relationships with other lay leaders. In this way you increase opportunity for yourself and for your congregation to be in ministry with others, and your credibility as a leader is enhanced.

Information on lay servant courses may be obtained through your district director of lay servant ministry, your district lay leader, district superintendent, conference director of lay servant ministry, or through the annual conference office. Lay servant print and downloadable resources are available from www.upperroombooks.org. For more information on Lay Servant Ministries go to www.gbod.org/laity.

CERTIFIED LAY MINISTER

On occasion, a district superintendent or bishop may assign a certified lay minister to provide pastoral leadership in a smaller congregation. The certified lay minister serves under the direction of a district superintendent or a supervising elder. Certified lay ministers may also serve in local churches in other roles to provide assistance to an appointed leader, such as for congregational care. Certified lay ministers complete courses beyond Lay Servant Ministries and are certified through the district committee on ordained ministry. For more information on certified lay ministry go to www.gbod.org/laity/clm.

Christian Conferencing/Leading Meetings

As a leader in your congregation, you will have the opportunity to lead meetings. It is important that we remember whom it is we are serving and whose work is to be done. Using a Christian conferencing format, consensus, and discernment is a way to keep Christ at the forefront of your meetings.

If you think about tithing your meeting time then **at least** six minutes of every hour should be set aside to honor Christ through prayer, singing, and biblical reflection. Think about ways that the atmosphere of your meetings could be changed by taking just a short time to include some of the means of grace. For example, light a candle to remind everyone of the presence of the light of Christ with you. Reserve an empty chair to represent Jesus' presence among you or use a symbol of the Holy Spirit, or a pitcher, bowl, and towel (signs of servanthood) before you as a reminder of your roles in Christ's church. Sharing prayer concerns at the beginning of the meeting can help members focus on the business at hand rather than on their problems at home, work, or school. Take time during your meetings to lift decisions in prayer before voting or getting consensus.

DISCERNMENT

Allow the Holy Spirit to guide your decisions. Discernment is listening for God's call or will—seeing the heart of the matter through spiritual eyes. Discernment is not new to the church. In 1 Samuel 16 the prophet Samuel discerned God's will regarding who would be anointed king. Acts 1:12-26; Romans 12:2; 1 Corinthians 12:10; and 1 John 4:1 also speak of discerning God's will. (See the Guidelines CD for more on a discernment process.)

CONSENSUS

Christian or holy conferencing is the manner in which we govern our lives together—it calls us to build each other up, not tear them down. In consensus we work together for the best possible decision for the group. The foundation for consensus rests in trust, respect, unity of purpose, non-violence, self-empowerment, cooperation, conflict resolution, commitment to the group, active participation, access to power, and patience. With the consensus model

- every interest is heard and understood
- everyone accepts the outcome—they may not agree with the decision but they agree to stand aside and not block the process
- all seek alternatives that address everyone's concerns and interests
- there is an obligation not to stymie, but to help the group meet your interests and needs
- there is an obligation to continue to try to meet the interests and needs of those who agree to stand aside
- there is group ownership of the decision
- if a vote is necessary to record numbers it can certainly be taken after consensus has been reached

MUTUAL INVITATION

Consider using a mutual invitation model during your meetings. This method involves an initial speaker presenting the agenda item or concern—speaking to it and then inviting someone else to speak. That person can either speak to the item or pass, but invites another person to speak. All persons have a chance to pass or speak in this model so that all have a chance to participate in the discussion.

INCLUSIVITY

When staffing committees, be inclusive in the representation. Include youth, young adults, older adults, men and women, and people of diverse ethnicities and abilities. Try to schedule meetings when persons of these groups would most likely be able to attend.

Communication Skills

One of the most difficult things to do is to listen. Active listening requires the full attention of everyone involved. Without listening, no communication takes place. The lay leader/lay member of annual conference listens to many different voices. In your role, you will hear from members of the congregation and from the pastor and staff. Some of these people may be angry or confused; some might have new ideas for ministry; and some want to tell you how they understand things. You may need to ask some quiet people for their opinions in interviews and surveys. Your active listening skills will be a key to your effectiveness as a leader of the congregation. The following are recommended guidelines for group interaction. Consider posting these guidelines in each area where meetings are held and call attention to them before beginning meetings.

RESPECTFUL COMMUNICATIONS GUIDELINES

R = Take **RESPONSIBILITY** for what you say and feel, without blaming others.

E = **EMPATHETIC** listening. Try to understand how the other person feels.

S = Be **SENSITIVE** to differences in communication styles.

P = **PONDER** on what you hear and feel before you speak.

E = **EXAMINE** your own assumptions and perceptions.

C = Keep **CONFIDENTIAL** what others have to say.

T = **TRUST** that God will speak to us in a way that each needs to hear.

(© Eric Law   www.ladiocese.org/ki. Used with permission.)

Leading Change

As lay leader/lay member of annual conference, you have responsibility to work with other leaders to guide your congregation through change. Change itself is not bad or good. It is part of life and growth. Congregations will welcome some changes, such as the need to add classes for new people and unexpected gifts to the budget. Some changes are not even noticed for a while, such as routine maintenance and a slow decline of Sunday school classes. Other changes are controversial and meet strong resistance—for example, a need to move the congregation or to add new worship forms or to become more welcoming. One of your leadership tasks is to work in partnership with other leaders to guide your congregation toward effective ministry with the current generation. The lay leader and pastor guide the congregation through appropriate change.

APPRECIATIVE INQUIRY AND ASSET DEVELOPMENT

One of the resources that can help you in the process of leading change is **Appreciative Inquiry (AI).** Most problem solving exercises focus on identifying a problem, analyzing the causes and possible solutions, and action planning that is better described as "treatment of the malady." In this process there is an assumption that the organization is or has a problem to be solved.

The Appreciative Inquiry process focuses on the positive things that have occurred or are occurring and builds on those. AI suggests that you look for what is working well in your congregation. What memories do you have of times when effective mission and ministry were happening? It bases the momentum for change on those high moments rather than what is *not* working right now. We have more confidence and comfort to journey to the future when we carry forward the good parts of the past. AI takes the focus off the problem and uses the positive energy from remembering the good to focus on what could be reality now and in the future. Appreciative Inquiry uses a cycle of processes that start with

- appreciating and valuing the best of "What Is"
- envisioning "What Might Be"
- dialoguing "What Should Be"
- innovating "What Will Be"

And then the cycle begins again as we discuss what is going well—valuing the best of what is, etc. (See Resources for more on Appreciative Inquiry.)

Another process that can help as we look at change is **Asset Based Community Development.** This concept considers how we work with other partners. Can one congregation do all the work of ministry in the community? Chances are that the answer is, "No!"

There are resources all around us if we are willing to consider visions of connecting with the community. Who has enough space for the community dinner to feed the hungry? It may not be your church, but another in the community or perhaps the YMCA. There may be partners in the community who would be willing to help fund or advertise ministries and missions within the community. Most often we focus on developing programs that give answers, identify needs, design a service, and make or serve "customers." What if we focused on people instead of programs, asked questions, identified gifts or motivations, mobilized action, and developed "citizens" instead of customers? How might our thinking change if we were willing to look beyond the walls and windows to the gifts and assets of the community beyond? And how much more could we accomplish in mission or service *with* those in need?

CONFLICT AND MEDIATION SKILLS
Turn problems into possibilities. Conflict is simply two different ideas in the same place at the same time. Conflict is the result of differences that produce tension, which is normal in communities and families. The important part of conflict management is bringing those conflicts into the open where they can be clarified.

The JUSTPEACE Center for Mediation and Conflict Transformation exists to prepare and assist United Methodists to engage in conflict constructively in ways that strive for justice, reconciliation, resource preservation, and restoration of community in the Church and in the world. The Center challenges leaders to prepare themselves for conflict transformation and then to engage others in transforming conflict. The Center summarizes the skills and attitudes needed for transforming conflict in its ten-point "Engage Conflict Well." This summary and other material is available by free download from http://www.justpeaceumc.org.

Evaluating Your Leadership

Sometimes we lose our way as we focus on various tasks to be completed during our ministry. And as a lay leader or lay member you have multiple responsibilities to keep on track. A way to do this is to set goals for the things that you expect to accomplish within a given time frame. When setting goals it is critical that they be specific and measureable—they need to state the criteria that indicate accomplishment. For instance, if your goal is to inform the laity of training events within the congregation, district, and annual conference—how will you know if you have accomplished that goal? The goal could state how often and in what manner you will inform the laity of training events. You could also set a goal for the number of people who actually attend the training after you have made them aware of it. An even better measure would be the results of their training, such as "After the announcement of the Lay Servant Ministries course on Discovering Your Spiritual Gifts, 10 people attended the course and 6 of them are now involved in different areas of mission or ministry where they are using their spiritual gifts."

You are encouraged to develop your own goals and measurements. Here are some samples to use as guidelines. For more information on evaluation and measurement please see the Guide to the Guidelines on the CD or "More on Measures and Evaluation: A Companion to the Vital Congregations Planning Guide." at www.umvitalcongregations.com.

Note that the samples include two or three suggested strategies, but measures for only one strategy.

SAMPLE: Goals and Measures Grid for *Lay Leader* at First UMC

REPRESENT THE LAITY	MODEL DISCIPLESHIP	MEET WITH THE PASTOR
DEFINITIONS: Serve as primary advocate for and representative of the laity in the congregation.	Model good habits of personal devotion and discipleship. Engage in spiritual practices and serve in outreach and mission.	Pastor and lay leader decide how they will guide the congregation together in accomplishing its mission
RESULTS: Laity know about and feel confident that their needs and concerns are accurately communicated to staff and congregational leaders	The congregation recognizes the lay leader's spiritual practices of discipline, devotion, and leadership both within and outside the church	The pastor and lay leader form a unified team who guide the church, with other leaders, in ministry within and beyond their church
STRATEGIES: R1. Set up listening posts for laity to share concerns or ideas for mission and ministry R2. Develop a communication tool to share these ideas with other leaders	MD1. Develop habits of personal devotion and corporate worship MD2. Engage in mission opportunities	MP1. Set a time for meetings with the pastor MP2. Draft a Leadership Covenant MP3. Develop a way to track discussions and results.
MEASURES: R2a. 50% of those issues/ideas were acted on by the pastor/staff/church council R2b. 90% of the leaders received the communication and acted on it.	MD1a. Spend time daily in devotions MD1b. Attend worship weekly unless prevented	MP2a. Covenant drafted within 30 days of lay leader's term MP2b. Covenant is reviewed or revised annually

SAMPLE: Goals and Measures Grid for *Lay Member* at First UMC

PREPARE FOR ANNUAL CONFERENCE SESSION	SERVE DURING CONFERENCE	REPORT TO THE CONGREGATION
DEFINITIONS: Study the pre-conference journal and materials that are submitted for action by the annual conference.	Participate in the annual conference sessions and vote on all matters except those pertaining to ministerial relations	Share information with your congregation about your experience,
RESULTS: Meet with the pastor, lay leader, and congregation members to discuss issues that will be a part of conference business	Attend the annual conference laity session through participation in all sessions dealing with annual conference business and worship, and voting when appropriate.	The congregation is informed about the annual conference proceedings, including decisions and policies that affect the church's ministry and administration, clergy expectations, resources for lay leadership, how "First UMC" members voted, worship ideas, and mission/ministry opportunities
STRATEGIES: P1. Attend Pre-conference sessions and read Journal P2. Relate proposed legislation to the *Discipline*	S1. Attend all sessions S2. Vote on legislation and recommendations S3. Journal business items, ideas, and other issues	R1. Work with the pastor to complete the report R2. Plan how to report with the chair of the council R3. Note items during church council and other committee meetings that may need to be taken to the annual conference
MEASURES: P1a. All pre-conference preparation is completed before the pre-conference sessions	S3a. Significant events and legislation noted in your journal on the same day S3b. Spoke to pastor and alternate to compare notes each day	R1a. By 7 days after conference, date set with pastor R1b. At meeting with pastor, date for congregational report set.

FOR REFLECTION

"And let us consider how we may spur one another on toward love and good deeds. Let us not give up meeting together, as some are in the habit of doing, but let us encourage one another..." (Hebrews 10:24-25, NIV).

- As a leader, what changes can you make in the way meetings are held in your church?
- What difference do you think it might make if all meetings were times of Christian conferencing?
- What results in your life have come from practicing spiritual disciplines? How have you seen those disciplines change and grow from your earliest efforts? What practices and processes have brought you to where you are now?
- As a leader, how will you encourage others to pursue the practice of spiritual disciplines in their lives?

A Final Word

Fulfilling these roles within the congregation gives you a wonderful opportunity to make a Kingdom impact! Become prepared spiritually to be the leader that God has called you to be. Open your eyes to the work of God in the world around you and discern how you can join God in that work. Encourage others in their various responsibilities within the church and assist them to become better equipped to be in mission in ministry in the world beyond the walls and windows of the church building.

May God be in your days.

A NOTE TO THE PASTOR

As the pastoral leader of your congregation you have the authority to guide and equip the members of your congregation to be in mission and ministry not only in the congregation but in their everyday lives. The responsibility of the local congregation is to make disciples who will be servants of Christ "on mission in the local and worldwide community. This servanthood is performed in family life, daily work, recreation and social activities, responsible citizenship, the stewardship of property and accumulated resources" and Creation (¶220 the *Book of Discipline*).

May God bless your efforts in this task.

Resources

CONNECTIONAL RESOURCES

The General Board of Discipleship provides consultation, training, research, print and electronic resources to enhance the ministry of congregations and church leaders. For more information and free resources, see the website at www.gbod.org and www.gbod.org/laity. An annual directory is available at annual conference or by calling (toll free) 1-877-899-2780, ext. 1793.

Director of Connectional Laity Development—General Board of Discipleship, 877-899-2780 ext. 7179

The Walk to Emmaus is a three-day experience exploring Christianity as a lifestyle. The Emmaus weekend is highly structured and is designed to strengthen and renew the Christian faith. For more information, go to www.upperroom.org/Emmaus.

The Academy for Spiritual Formation is an experience of disciplined Christian community for laity and clergy that emphasizes holistic spirituality—nurturing body, mind, and spirit. There is a 2-year Academy experience or a 5-day Academy. See http:www.upperroom.org/academy.

Many conferences and districts offer regular or occasional training, renewal events, mission trips, and other resources for local church leadership. Contact your district office and ask to be put on the mailing list for information or check the conference website.

GENERAL RESOURCES

The Book of Discipline of The United Methodist Church 2012, (Nashville: The United Methodist Publishing House, 2012.

The United Methodist Hymnal (Nashville: The United Methodist Publishing House, 1989. ISBN pew edition blue 978-0-687-33044-7) and *The United Methodist Book of Worship* (ISBN 978-0-687-03572-4).

LEADERSHIP

Learning & Leading courses (including *Lay Servant courses*) can be used in many venues (small groups, Sunday school classes, etc.) to equip all laity as they grow in their discipleship and ministry. *www.upperroom.org.* The **Lay Ministry Equipping Resources** catalog can be ordered by calling